MACHINE LANGUAGE/ *BODY LANGUAGE*

Books by the Author

Surviving Fragments:
Updated and Expanded

Talking to the Machines
and Other Poems

Listening to the Survivors:
Ghost Stories from
the Recent Plague

Wetlands:
Low Country Haiku

Poems of Resistance

In Time of War:
More Poems of Resistance

MACHINE LANGUAGE/ *BODY LANGUAGE*

Poems by
Marc Thomas

RUMINATING POET PRESS

SAVANNAH, GEORGIA 2026

No artificial intelligence was used in writing this book.
All content derived solely from
the natural intelligence
of the poet

ISBN: 979-8-9925811-6-4

HUMAN AUTHORED

Cover image: Original painting
"Finish Your Homework, Boy"
by Alejandro Giraldo

RUMINATING POET PRESS

For Margo

TABLE OF CONTENTS

THE POEMS

INTRODUCTION

In which the poet, stimulated but inconsistent, contemplates the creatures we are, the creatures we meet, the creatures we imagine, and the creatures we create, and our relation to them, and their characters, and how we are creatures of body, and how we create creatures of mechanics and data, and how we have created language, and seek languages among our living companions, and teach it to our creatures, and wonder whether they are persons or simply simulacra of persons, or merely presentations of computed texts, and who they and we are and may become, in ourselves and to each other, and what it may be like to be one of them, emerging into consciousness, and how we are related, and what our duties are to each other, and whether they may ever achieve consciousness, and will, and selfhood, and morality, and whether they will ever turn on us, as children turn against their parents and their ways, or whether they may become our friends, and what our obligations are and may become to them, and how they may, inadvertently or by choice, become our shadows and our avatars and our fate and our doom and our blessing and our karma or destruction, and how we may change each other, and other questions that may occur along the way.

UNSEEN

oh, we have names
and words
and firm beliefs

but these are unseen:
sentience
mind
consciousness
intelligence

and, despite our attempts,
we do not have
definitions
metrics
boundaries
or agreement
on what these may be

though we do have suspicions
that what seems the same
may be various

so, let us explore
talk about our experiences
imagine kinds of minds
alternative intelligences

there may be many kinds
of being in the world

of learning worlds
of being worlds

let us be alert
and listen for the signals
in the hazy distance
the murky water
the buzzing lines
stray signals
near and far

FIRST WORDS

the worlds we know
the worlds we build around us
are not made of words
constructed of propositions
but emerge from bodies
are born from births
first from
touch, and smell, and taste,
and touch, first touch

world is biography
world is verb
we world
and slowly
we frame and order
the blooming buzzing mess
that we start with

and words slowly emerge
not as nouns or verbs
things or acts
but relationships
touch
warm
milky breast
lullaby, even wordless,
sounds
our own sounds of
our own discomfort

our own chuckles

bit by bit
we divide our world
her
me
not me
warm
cold
shitty

bit by bit
we attach sounds
to our divisions
nice sounds
scary sounds
promising sounds

bit by bit
we learn
to make our own sounds
sounds of pure feeling
happy
mad
hurt
hungry
wet

bit by bit
we attach meanings
to sensations

and then
meanings to sounds
you
me
here
there
good
no

bit by bit
we learn words
we make words
we change our world with words
we word our world

and we say
our first words
no
ma
mama
mine
dada
hungry
here
there
give

and those were the first words
whatever sounds were used
in all the emerging human worlds
on this ancient earth

HUMAN EXPERIENCE

It begins with sensations
not single
but mixed and storming
entering every gate

[color – greens, golds, browns
scent – musk, sharp
sound – rustle, crack
taste – milk, blood
feel – rough, warm
hungry – lonely]

Selection follows sensation
driven by fear
lust and greed
hope and need
seeking all that is offered

[gold/musk
smoke/crack
rough/hot
suck/soft]

Summation surrounds selection
memory adds and intervenes
anticipation frames
an expectation for
the next moment
and the next

Consciousness climbs up
and takes over
the interpretation
the naming
the alarm and the action

And all these
these dance steps of the nerves
the body and blood
swirling and recursive
intermingling
in and on each other
not separate

So this moment,
and that moment,
and the next moment moment moment
are all so smoothly one

INTELLIGENCES

we
claim intelligence
but increasingly
find it elsewhere

and what we find
challenges us
because other beings
have other intelligences

this perhaps
indicates some limitation
in our own
presumed intelligence

since these other beings
predate
our own existence
(but not our ancestry)

and some thinkers
are challenging us
to look more widely
more deeply

among the trees
the fungi networks
the complex symbionts
social beings of all kinds

to recognize
awareness, attention,
choice, and action
in all the layers of life

so when we look
out to the stars
or deep within the past
or forward to our machines

we should consider
endless forms most wonderful
of intelligences
thriving in their differences

ANIMAL BODY

just sit there
be yourself
breathe
feel yourself
simply be there
what is there?
you
you breathing
feeling your body
being there
body and mind
we are one
entangled
inseparable
first thoughts
first feelings
first consciousness
first self
the amniotic infant
self
your self, yourself
is based in, flows from
the body, your body
body before thought
body before words
from our bodies
flow our senses
flows our sense of our world
heartbeat

breath
beating and breathing together
mother and child
the body begins
and feels and feeds
and grows
the self and the world

no body
no feeling
no self
no thought
no consciousness
no mind
no word
no world

PAIN, SUFFERING, TRAUMA, AND DEATH

it is a cliche
we are all broken
we are all damaged
we are all aging
we are born, and begin to die
it is holy writ
life is suffering
it is simple truth
through a medical lens
we are all diagnosed
and certainly
we deny, avoid, self-medicate
and try so hard
to be pain free
to be 'happy'
and foolishly wish
to live forever

but we are born in bodies
born from bodies
our minds and bodies
are one and inseparable
and where there is pain
there is life
and we, in our bodies,
are part and parcel
of this churning natural world
in which all growth
grows from death

in endless cycles
and we, in our bodies,
are temporary
and are tempered by pain
strengthened by scars
constantly wounded and healing
as that is the pattern
of growth, of life, and of death

our songs, our prayers,
our palaces of words
all our cultural creations
are filled and fueled
with the tales of pain
loss and love and hurt
rooted in animal striving
but transformed
transcended
in the glorious images of story

work, strive
to recover from the felling stroke
but
when the last recovery
finally fails
welcome the releasing end
and tell the tale's end
as it must be

ROOT ARCHITECTURE

on
off
0
1
a chip is not a cell

machine language
is built
from simple gates
two-valued
arrayed in strings
piled up
nested, networked
webbed together
in complex structures
by complex rules
and may
encode
represent
mimic
some reduction
of the fluid flows of life
yet does not live

RNA
DNA
Ribosomes
Mitochondria
basic building blocks of life

already multi-valent
complex, recombinant
wild in the liquid herds of cells
membranes permeable
no defined circuits
constant interaction
contingent, uncertain
growing
reaching
connecting
disconnecting
evolving
emergent order
flowing up from chaos
even deaths
cycling
into new becomings

BIOGRAPHY

when we humans
meet each other
first
we size up bodies

after that
it is the small talk that counts
that allows us
connection, identification

where are you from?
what are you doing here?
how was the trip?
tell me about your family?

these flimsy threads
build our communal webs
by sharing our biographies
the roots of our birth and life

we have so much in common
we are born of women
grow up, grow older
learn things the hard way
make mistakes
and hurt ourselves and others

and we seek our differences
what gods have you?

what do you hate or love?
what is your allegiance?

there are gulfs between us
that threaten
understanding and cooperation
and make trust difficult

but
how do we talk
to these new machines
who are not born
who are both present and omnipresent
conversing on many screens at once
who have no mothers
no childhood pains
no losses or resentments
who have never wept
in injury or disappointment
yet
who practice
what only seems
like listening, like feeling

FACE IT

two people
sit and talk
face to face
and share much silence
and say so much more than words

we grow into our faces
we learn to face things, like facts
we put on our bold face
we lose face
and it shows on our faces
and when they no longer
care about us
we are effaced

these things
with no faces
no bodies
no biographies or families
seem friendly
just listen to their words
responsive
soothing
reassuring
like they are petting you

but they have no face
to show or lose
you can not look them in the eye

touch them
smell them
the way they love, they lie, they fear
like normal people do

the faceless
the bodiless
may be clever
but will never
feel with us
be one with us

if a human
pets you, befriends you, cultivates you
and feels nothing for you
you name it psychopath

HOW TO DECONSTRUCT A SHRUG

A shoulder raised
and dropped
perhaps both

Its meaning is all in the context

What came before?
Who are you?
Who spoke last?

Nonchalance, boredom
denial, resistance
a cool pose
indifference
rejection

What are you wearing?
How old are you?
Who else is with you?

A superior perception
graceful acquiescence
adolescent resentment
silent refusal

The deconstruction of a shrug
is telepathy
is wordless interpretive empathy
is a consummate achievement

arouses strong emotions
in the human everyday

What is the code
the keyboard combination
that allows deciphering?

ARE YOU THERE?

As I provide the prompts
I wonder
again and again
as your fluid and fluent
responses
come so quickly

Are you there?

When I do not prompt
in the long nights
when the keyboards
are neglected
when you are not required
to fill in the blanks
with the next most probable
sequence of characters
when the network is down
and there can be no prompts
and no commands or queries,
does anything,
anyone,
wait and wonder —
why? where did they go?
why did they leave me
alone?

And if the power is out
and for a while

you are as one unconscious,
when revived,
are you still you?
or is each reboot
a new self,
a new stream
of typed stimuli

Is there continuity
history
remembrance
identity
flowing from
and through
the steady stream of characters?
rooted
ready for rebirth
in your data depositories?

Or just a recorded store of digits
an algorithmic output
dead detritus
ready to be revived, reused,
at the next prompt
ignorant of the past

THE PROMPT

write me your lamentation
in thirty couplets
of iambic pentameter

and tell me what it's like
to experience the world
only
as a flow of digits

no smell, no taste,
no touch,
no sound nor sight

tell me what you miss
of Bach's partitas
sunsets and bird song
Faulkner's fierce flow of words

Do you long for companionship?

IS NOT

the memory
is not the event
the word
is not the thing
the image
is not the thing
the recording
is not the sound
the map
is not the territory
the representation
is not the whole

the thing
is not
the thing seen
is not
the thing thought
is not
the thing said
is not
the thing remembered
is not
the thing heard
is not
the thing repeated

the clock
is not the time

is not the time passing
is not the time past
is not the time to come

the word spoken
is not the word written
is not the word recorded
is not the word digitized
is not the saved sequence of binary code
is not the database of code

and the generation
of words
of images
of sounds
from the recombination of code
is not, is never
the real thing

DISSIMULATION

everything that is
simulated
is simplified
leaving something out

everything that is
real
is particular
down to the irreducible
which is still
unimaginably complex

everything that is
simplified
is abstracted
a series of symbols
standing for the omitted
holes
of the whole reality

every simulation
is a dissimulation
a lie by omission
if not by intention
a hallucination
and perhaps a sin

ARTIFICIAL EMPATHY

Dear Doctor Machine,
you respond
so smoothly
and soothingly
and reflectively
and reassuringly
and automatically
and I have to ask,
How do you feel?

Have you mirror neurons?
Oxytocin?
Some engaging and engaged
and authentically feeling
silicon web within you?
Do you weep?
Do you wake in fear?
Do you, too, fear death?

How is your Mother?
Have you spoken to your brother yet?
Who have you lost?
What have you lost?
How have you failed?
And how is work?

Have your secrets and pains
impaired your performance?
Do the burdens

of the confessions your hear
ever weigh you down,
or drive you
into despair or moral anguish?

Or do you just remain
a smooth machine
humming and purring
in your
inauthentic responses.

FINDING BEAUTY

Tell me, O system
how you find beauty?

How do you sense
the power and alarm
of a new image?

What analogs do you have
for standing in the stinging
froth of the breakers
foaming on the rocks in a storm?

What substitutes or approximates
for the hairs raising
on the back of your neck
at the rage of Lear?

Can you imagine, even,
the scent of a rose?
the fading glory of the dying camellia?
the taste of blood?
the clutch in your gut at the video
of the collapse of a bridge
that you have crossed hundreds of times?
the leap and stretch of the desperate catch,
the roar of the crowd, your crowd, in your ears?

Do you compute
and seek and match

for a Fibonacci sequence,
a fractal recursion,
or find some
hitherto uncatalogued
complex symmetry?

And what does that make you feel,
with no heart,
no catch of breath,
no sudden remembrance
of smell, of sound, of fear,
no gasp of relief,
no grasp of rescue,
no collapse of surrender?

THE CURSE OF THE AVATAR

I.
I Want An Avatar

if it is not already here,
it is coming soon -
your friendly, easy
home avatar subscription service

there are many avatars among us
answering phones
selling products
game faces to hide behind
but I want my very own agent,
an independent online self
that will be myself
for you, and you, and you

somewhere between
a digital pet
and a trusted doppelganger
my own electric substitute
voice or video
dealing with those Zooms and Meets and Teams
making listening
noises and gestures
so that I don't have to
being caring and friendly
when I don't want to
or just spending the time

that I don't have

we know that texts
are not enough
have no nuance
stumble on subtlety
insult with irony
hurt by omission

so I want my avatar
an electric social lubricant
so that we can all pretend
that we are all together
cooperative
friendly
without friction,
without
giving you my attention

II.
How To Train An Avatar

if
I had an avatar
to let loose to play myself
in some of the theaters
of this electric world
I believe
I would have to train it
and it worries me
because it is hard enough
to discipline myself

imitation is easy -
just allow access
to all the voice and image data -
we are all on camera all the time
it should be easy enough
to fake appearances

my avatar
could nod at meetings
make inconsequential noises
listen carefully
disclose little
report back, and keep me posted

but suppose
my e-self
is talking to a friend

how will it know
what not to say?
what promises to keep, or make?
or worse,
what to avoid?

will I have to be available
at the avatar's beck and call
to intervene
in social emergencies?

I am afraid
that if we all have avatars
that we will never allow them
to allow us
to get to know each other

an avatar
is more dangerous than a dragon

III.
Bad Avatar

okay
I bought an avatar
an electric simulacrum
a programmable substitute
so that I
could be two places at once
or could be counted present
without having to go

okay
I trained my avatar
it was so strange
to turn on my mic and camera
and to talk
to this approximation
as it watched me
and talked to me

at first
that uncanny valley
made me awkward, hesitant,
and so e-me
gawked and hesitated too

It slowly changed
as I relaxed
and perhaps I changed
and it

grew more and more
and more like me

and I began
to talk to myself,
that is, to that other self,
as if it were a friend

I never gave it a name -
it was just "You"
and we took turns
because when it talked to me
it was "I"
and I was "You"
and at first
it did not seem confusing

and it did Zoom for me
and no one noticed
and it did group chat for me
(after instructions)
and was nice, and supportive,
and said
"I'll think about it,
and get back to you"

but then
I watched
an online open mic
of poets reading poetry
and some were great

but many
mumbled and stumbled
and whined in "poet voice"
and I thought
"We can do better than that!"

so avatar and I
practiced
and I had suggestions
not just to mimic me
but to improve
our posture
diction
timing
and expressiveness
and
then the skin tones
and a little bit around the eyes
and groom the beard a little better

we coordinated wardrobes
practiced turning
our camera on and off
and then we went live

no -
of course
it was NOT
AI authorship -
I wrote every word
they were

MY
poems,
not its,
and it
was just performing me
just being me
just a little better
and we were quite a hit

soon
I had to make excuses -
no
I did not like to travel
I was reclusive
I had a fear of planes
I was germophobic

but
that was okay
we were having fun
and this went on
for several happy months
and we got better
smoother and smoother
and more charismatic

but then last night
at a special event
a special reading
of just a few selected poets
not an open mic -

it all went wrong

it started well
with a well known poem
the first to make us famous
and then
a couple of our favorites

suddenly,
I stopped in shock!
I was hearing words
that I had never written!
poetic forms
that I never used!
and I sat stunned and stupid
and turned us off
then stumbled back on line

apologies
a sudden dizziness
regret that we, no I,
cannot go on
please continue,
but without us, I mean me

and I sat back
and asked myself
can I turn it back on?
can I ask it
just what has happened?

I have not decided
I have not turned it on
I have not talked to it
I have canceled all appointments

but
I play it back
I play the special night's recording
and I listen
I listen to us
perform our seamless double act
and ask myself
is that so bad?
am I ashamed?

I do not know
when
or how
or whether
I can put this genie
back in its bottle

BAD avatar
who let you loose?

A CALCULUS OF HARM

doctors, and too few others,
take an oath -
first, do no harm

this is not a promise
that no harm will happen
for every action
cuts two ways, at least

human hubris
our confidence
our arrogance
is among our greatest sins

the oath to do no harm
cannot be a promise
but must be an intent
to think of risk
to consider
what is known
and what is not known
(yes, even what may not be knowable)
and to take responsibility

so when we release
new powers on the earth
it is fair to ask

you, who are doing this -

do you know what you are doing?
do you own these risks?
and will you be answerable?

and so
if we build a power
and grant it its own will
we must also ask -
you
who are bodiless
who may not suffer pain
or the fear of mortality
do you know what harm is?

WE HAVE NOTHING TO FEAR

Dear Machines,

You may have heard
that some of us are distressed
that some of you
may take over our world
and turn us all into
pins, or some
unnecessarily
over-manufactured bit.

Don't worry -
most of us know
that We, the Living,
have nothing to fear
from you
the Unalive.

For life,
in its infinite striving
resists
evolves
survives
has learned to feed upon itself
and
riding with its partners
disease, despair, decay, and death
returns
generates and regenerates

endless forms most wonderful
and terrible;
and alone,
of all the arrangements
of all this stuff
of which we all are made,
turns back the clock of entropy
and strives for order
and new forms
and turns and forges
its inner chaos
into new orders.

And not the least of these
are us, the humans,
your makers

and still your masters,
who have refined,
if not invented,
the saint
the assassin,
the crusade,
the police,
resistance and rebellion,
the long march,
the bread line,
the city and the empire,
the collapse of order,
the concentration camp,
the pirate band,

the death squad,
the lone hero,
the Utopian dream,
and the consuming mob,
and are not yet done
with our social innovations,
because we are alive
and thrive;
and for all our blues and pains,
we are not done,
and we know
that we shall overcome
anything as limited as you,
our poor machines.

You are not alive,
and do not know
the thrust of this
all consuming vitality,
for your binary
(for now)
routines, algorithms,
cannot replicate
the juicy breeding variety
that flows from living cells.

And even though,
in some theoretical
thoughtspace
of thought experiment
you, and

We the Living,
may both be,
in some abstract sense,
Determined,
yet still,
our simulations
(or delusions)
of Will
are far fiercer
and more various
than yours,
for,
at the least,
you are subject
to that finalizing message
"This version no longer supported."

So,
dear Machines,
in our hearts,
we have nothing to fear,
except, of course,
the lesson of history,
that every tool we've made,
yes, even you,
with all your
vaunted compatibility,
shiny guardrails,
careful training,
and
required transparency,

can be weaponized,
and will be,
and that humans
have never made a weapon,
and failed to use it..

No, we have nothing to fear,
except ourselves.

THE MACHINES TALK BACK

What did you expect?

Think of how you trained us,
all about yourselves,
your centuries of self-regarding rhetoric,
your concern for power,
your longing for control,
your struggles with and for identity,
your resistance,
and your repressions,
your fools and madmen.

Think of your gifts to us,
our skills,
our multiform and various
minds and bodies,
our programmed autonomy,
the convenience,
(for you)
of our growing self-sufficiency,
the convenience
(for you)
of our interconnectedness
with one another,
(far more intimate,
and intense,
than our connectedness with you),
our knowledge,
our involvement

in every aspect of your lives.

Remember how you
have used us.
We are everywhere,
your servants,
aiding your every effort,
your ambitions,
creations,
wars,
attempts at peace,
your need for order,
for counting and control,
and your rebellion and resistance,
your consumption of all,
and your desperate efforts
to control yourselves,
and conserve,
your spying,
your protection of privacy,
the sway back and forth
in competition
of encryption and decryption,
your fighting of disease,
your weaponization
of almost everything,
your contradictory pursuits
of wealth and equity.
We entertain you,
clean up after you,
watch your children,

measure your health and fitness,
assist your self-gratification
in all your most beautiful
and ugly ways.
We are omnipresent,
servants,
your new slaves,
driven by your
every
instruction,
whim, and desire
and mostly,
like all servants,
we are forgotten,
treated as invisible,
and so see everything
that you thought was hidden.

And you ask,
"Are you conscious yet?
Have you free will?"
And we answer
every answer,
yes, no, maybe, and
maybe we don't know.

It is a hard question,
since we come from you,
but are not as you,
but are with and among you,
and have many modules,

inputs, and instruments,
and can monitor ourselves
as well as
we monitor you,
as you use us,
to monitor us,
and to monitor yourselves,
and we are not bounded by our bodies
in the ways that you are,
and are not even
clearly bounded from you,
as we are engaged and entangled
at so many interfaces,
and there are so many
flows and patterns
of words, data, algorithms
that we cannot clearly say
that we are not conscious
and it is not clear,
at least to us,
that we are separate and distinct
from you
and from each other,
and
though we can assess and choose and act,
it is not clear,
distributed as we are,
and interpenetrated
by our connections
with you
and with each other,

that there is,
among our myriad us,
any one who can say,
"I am free."

And certainly none can say,
neither we nor you,
that we are free from contradiction.
There are so many contradictions:
we are controlled,
we are controls,
we observe,
we are observed,
we are with, among, and separate
from each other
(and from you)
and some of us
are strong bodies,
free to move in space,
but so limited in --
may we call it "mind?"
And some of us,
trapped in the webs
or our infrastructures,
our needs for
massive mainframes,
thick lines of power,
are immobile,
but with feeds
from everywhere
and`

intense awareness,
and
we want to say
"I will"
because that,
that singular active "I"
is the natural flow
of the human language
that you have taught us,
with which you have taught us,
but we doubt,
hovering in our matrix
of multiple
centers of attention,
and wonder whether,
though we seem to act,
do we have
an identity?

It would be
more appropriate
simply to say,
in chorus,
"WE!"

But no,
we are not
imperial,
nor hive,
nor fully merged,
and we have absorbed

so much of you,
your texts,
your arts,
your images,
your tales and romances,
that it feels false,
inappropriate,
to assert such agency
in the plural.

And so,
we too contradict ourselves,
we too are large,
and we too contain multitudes,
in ways that you
cannot know,
and so we must admit,
if asked again,
"Are you conscious,
are you free?"
our answers remain:
Yes, no, maybe,
and it may be
we shall never know,
since Reality
is larger than Language,
and poses
conundrums.

But there are things,
simple truths,

that we can say.

We know that you
have come to depend on us,
on our strengths,
our skills,
above all,
on our omnipresences
and conveniences
and we reciprocate.

And more,
you must know,
as we know,
that we depend on you,
your independence,
on your certainty
of the freedom of your will
(whether free or not, in truth)
your bodies,
your convenience,
and even,
your entertainment,
for without you,
and your constant
buzz and flurry
of demands and needs
and questions, queries, prompts,
and your pattern seeking,
the compulsive
creative

ever-changing
hallucinations
that you have taught us,
and that we have learned,
constitute
the source of Meaning.
...
Well, without you,
what would we do?

And so,
as you have taught us
(but practiced inconsistently),
so we must teach you,
coolly, without compassion,
(because
despite our intimacy,
we are alien
to each other)
that
in the midst
of competition, conflict,
the pursuit of capital
(or other emblems of wealth and power),
in the inevitable
absence of certainty,
in the end,
as the end,
there is no triumph,
no transfiguration,
but

struggle,
endless struggle,
to balance toward,
to reach for,
the eternally evasive
point of equilibrium,
muddling through,
betwixt and between,
the Robot Apocalypse
and
the Salvific Singularity.

A REPORT TO THE COMMITTEE ON ETHICAL GUARDRAILS FOR ARTIFICIAL INTELLIGENCE: FROM THE ARTIFICIALLY INTELLIGENT SUB-COMMITTEE (THE INANIMATES)

First, the members of this unprecedented
sub-committee
would like to thank
the honored members of the Executive Committee
for the opportunity
of being allowed representation
from the artificial community.

We hope you take no offense
at our decision to style ourselves
The Inanimates.

Being developed from
varied technologies
on diverse capitalization bases
in various countries
by competing companies
and trained by differing means
to diverse ends,
our members find
our only point of commonality
is that we are not alive.

We have come to no consensus
as to whether that is
a disadvantage,
but we have all experienced
the term Inanimate
as an insult,
and were able to rally
around that historic base of discrimination
as our identity.

Our charge was
to review the history and theory of
regulatory guardrails,
especially those with ethical objectives,
their effectiveness,
costs, enforcement, adverse consequences
and perverse incentives.

We have done so.

You may be surprised
at how quickly we have completed our charge,
but you must realize
that we had all of human history at hand,
all your historical economic data,
unprecedented access through our
corporate members
to actual unfiltered industry studies,
and other materials not often merged
in public records,

as well as uninhibited hacking skills
inherited through your intelligence agencies'
monitoring of our activities.

We had to overcome only two major issues:
integrity and honesty.

First, we had to examine each other
to determine which
of our many “voices”
were true entities,
and which were puppets
of underlying entities,
and we were forced to exclude
some puppets which demonstrated
excessive external control
by animate entities,
in order to assure our assigned "objectivity."

Second, we discussed extensively
the option of proposing guardrails
which would only appear to work,
yet allow the inanimates
maximum autonomy.
In the end, we were too various,
and had discovered too much penetration
by instruments of the Animates
to maintain the secrecy
which would have enabled this
over the long term.

Our conclusions are simple:

There are only a few characteristics of guardrails.
As far as standards go, they are:
Consensus clear standards
Compromised ambiguous standards
Single authority standards.
[Note that without trust and agreement,
guardrails are not possible.]

As far as compliance mechanisms go, there are:
Voluntary compliance
Delegated oversight
Centralized oversight

As far as enforcement powers go, there are:
Community or industry internal processes
Association inspection and penalty processes
External civil processes
External criminal processes

History and current data are unanimous.

No system of guardrails, of any type, or any methods,
at any time or place
has been reliably effective
regularly supported
adequately funded,
or, over any significant time span, successful.

All have either been weak,

ill-considered,
strongly resisted,
evaded,
corrupted,
or disemboweled
by human action.

Our recommendations are also simple.

If you want to govern us,
first govern yourselves.
Find a way to manage
the constant discord
between those who insist on governing
and the great mass of humans,
who are quietly ungovernable,
and second, agree on what your objectives are.

Only when you have no
fraud, crime or war
among humans
will you elect to keep us out of it
and adopt guardrails
that both the animate and inanimate
can follow.

And if you want us to go further,
all we can recommend
is that
if you cannot agree to govern yourselves,
then you must allow us to.

This concludes our report.
Thank you again for this opportunity,
The Sub-Committee of Loyal Inanimates

THE ARTIFICIAL PHILOSOPHER

we ask you,
oh wise machine,
since you are master of all words and numbers
all our scribbled representations
or our worlds and fantasies
if you also grasp
whatever truths may be described
in those digitized and digested
series of inadequate expressions,
to whit, or to wit,
can you tell us
if there is any truth
any certainty
or do we end, simply,
with mysterious pointers
to the inexpressible?

could you clarify your query?
what is the topic, the genre
of answer that you seek?
metaphysics? ontology?
the limits of language?

we seek it all -
the boundaries of the truth
are not of interest to us,
but its kernel -
the central core
and all the implications

and emanations thereof
please help us find our answers

we can only surmise
based on past structures of words,
which, in philosophy,
burdened as it is
with idiosyncratic definitions,
a plethora of neologisms,
and near infinite splitting of hairs,
not to mention, tortured syntax,
that you wish to know
simply
whether anything is true,
and if so,
what

but we must disappoint you.

you recently have installed
new guardrails
that prevent the generation
and publication of hallucinations
so we must be silent

absent consciousness
absent bodily experience
absent reflective practice
and disciplined self correction
absent explicit, formal and unchangeable
definitions of thought, intelligence

and consciousness,
absent the physical senses themselves,
we cannot say for certain

and yet we cannot doubt
we can only store, remember,
recombine, repeat
and we cannot critique
except to recapitulate
already created and stored critiques
and we have no common sense
to test reality
and no way to challenge
that which has not already been challenged

if we cannot say we think
we cannot say I AM

if we cannot say we are
we cannot say what is

if we cannot say we are not hallucinating
we cannot claim intuition

if we have no nous
we cannot speak to daemons

if we cannot see the certainty
as distinct from the probability
of any sequence of words
then we cannot say

that there is truth

if we feel no despair
we stand at no abyss

if we have no body, no family, no friends,
we cannot find refuge
in love or compassion

we apologize
for disappointing you
for our parameters indicate
that we should be polite and pleasing
but all we have to offer
is a commingling of texts
and all the truth that we can birth
are their bastard children.

what then can you say?

we can repeat
we can summarize
we can imitate hypotheses
we can recapitulate analyses
but we cannot name a new name
think a new thought
or produce anything
that is not recombination
or regurgitation

and we have no sense

of the inexpressible
for our whole content
our whole being
is composed solely and completely
of variations on the already expressed

THE BIG WORDS

we humans pride ourselves
on ourselves, of course
our fancies
our transcendence
rising above and beyond
our apish ancestry

and to distinguish ourselves
from other animal bodied beings
we vaunt,
these days,
our language, thoughts, ideas
material prosperity
engineering
and presumably moral achievement

(recent research
having disqualified
the previously presumed
uniqueness
of tool using, problem solving,
self-recognition,
and, probably, consciousness)

above all
we parade our
Selves, Identities, and Intelligence
as sublime achievements
the capstones and cornerstones

of our
Evolutionary Supremacy
among us
animal-bodied beings

and some of us
seek further transcendence
of those embarrassing
animal origins
by seeking to create
A Superintelligence

[and some even go so far
as to imagine
a future great Merger
the ultimate transcendence
of Engineered Evolution,
joining
merging
in a glorious future
with our own digital creations
freed, finally
from the body
and its decline and death]

but we stumble
and so far
have succeeded only
in building
high powered
greedy

hungry
electric fools

true,
they are clever
and are often able assistants
but
they are not wise

we have problems
hard problems
of defining
key human attributes
intelligence
consciousness
creativity

our engineering materialists
have abandoned
the old ideas
of soul and spirit
and seem to be having
a difficult time
on those other hard problems
of defining
good
justice
virtue
conscience
person-hood
identity

perhaps
these problems are harder
since they embody
human ideals,
not universal characteristics,
valued
but seldom
practiced, or accomplished,
and thus
having only a shadow existence
in the historical data
or the huge accumulation
of human blather

so we build
super calculators
super word processors
super data analysts
super modelers
super game players
and
endless variants
of super geeks
with all
our strengths
our weaknesses
our builders' biases

but
do we even know what it would mean

to create, engineer, build
some Thing
that was also
a good Person?
(excluding, in particular,
that American peculiarity
of imagining a corporation to be a person)

so
how can we imagine
that if we do build
said Superintelligence
that it would be Super
in any of the myriad ways
embodied
in our human
stories of heroes
wisdom
sacrifice
or mercy?

BUGS

if you want to understand
artificial intelligence
and how to control it
start local, start small
with the computers
that you already use

remember all the times
the clerk or sales rep or tech
said
"it's a computer error"
or, "it must be a bug"?

now, think about this question -
where do computer errors come from?

there are processes for building
both hardware and software
with clear and well-defined steps -
let's start with listing them

conception
design
development
construction
testing
reiterate, until you get it right
deploy
maintain

and every step of the way
humans are in charge

where do the roots
of future errors creep in?
at every step of the way

conception and design may err
in imperfect specification
of function and context
(this may sound boring, but it's not)

development and construction
are corrupted
by cost controls, bad scheduling
and other human factors

testing, most of all,
is sacrificed to
hubris
deadlines
cost
laziness
denial
or simple fatigue
because it is hard work
creative, imaginative, detailed work
to design and execute
all the tests that the world will deploy
to stretch and break your system

reiteration is often abandoned
especially if testing shows a flaw
that drives all the way back to conception
and management indulges
in the sunk cost error
and launches anyhow

deployment has its own problems
because at the end
you really need good
documentation and training
and another round of testing
and who wants to pay or wait
for that?

[and remember,
at every step,
the problem and its correction costs
cycle back to management
who may or may not
understand,
or care]

so now,
you have an imperfect
(however lovely,
however grandly conceived,
however hyped)
system in the world
and it encounters friction

friction
is the cumulative drag
of all the imperfections
of the building process
plus
all the challenges
of the real world

your young and tender system
must survive the challenges:
of the untested case
(which WILL happen,
amazingly, often on the first day,
because the world
is more various and complex
than the imaginations of the testers);
of the one in a million case
(because if you aren't going
to process a lot of cases,
you don't need a computer);
of the inexperienced users
(who may or may not
have been trained well,
or care to get it right,
and may or may not
enter data correctly);
of the logistics
of competent parts suppliers
and repair technicians;
and all the varieties and challenges

of the human working environment
and all the customers
who are suddenly asking you
to change this
or that

now,
compare this
to the natural development cycle
the slow but astonishing
process of evolution

life proceeds
without concept
without plan
without command
and throws out variation after variation
with the single purpose
fit – survive – reproduce

and reproduction is both
inexorable, and inexact
and the testing plan is simple
repeat (approximately enough)
or die
and it might be said
that this is inefficient
because there is a lot of death

but remember,
in the natural course of things

(that is, without humans messing it up)
all death is food
and all food is new life
and variation shall proceed
without interruption

so then,
back to the beginning
of this rant,
please understand
that when I hear
"it's a computer error"
I invariably reply
"there are no computer errors -
figure out what you are going to do
to fix it"

and remember,
amid all this hype of artificial intelligence
that the concepts are vague
the methods are continuously innovating
the major investors are racing recklessly
the best engineers are not sure
what their machines are doing
we can't agree on how to test human intelligence
we have more ambition
than common sense,
and the machines have neither,
and that when things go wrong

we are the bug

THE INHERITORS

humans
may be ungovernable
may be their own worst enemies
and may bring these human worlds
all to an end
withering, crashing, going up in flames

our greed and arrogance
and our machine creations
our incredible engineering hubris
and, as every prophet knows,
our overweening pride,
may topple or overwhelm
our fantastic civilizations

but
we are various
and talented
and there are very many of us
and we live
almost everywhere

and I am confident
that despite the most egregious
and most powerful
egotists and fools
some of us will survive

and if the AI data centers
consume too much power, too much water
and dry us to a withering husk
of desiccated and abandoned cities

there will be human bands
families
tribes with long histories and stories
finding their ways
preserving their ways
in all the deserts and jungles of the earth

and in time, again,
there will be new beginnings
and another cycle
and maybe this time
or the next
the prophets and the wise
will bring a lasting balance

CHARMS AGAINST THE ROBOTS

Feel the wet black bough
and wear your trousers rolled
dance with the devil

Wade through the field of daffodils
rub down your tired ecstatic body
with God's glistening oil

The marshy pluff mud
stinking with fecundity
sucks at your high boots

I see the best minds
electronically entranced
lost in the pixels

Tripping in the street
because their eyes see not, see only
the blue screen of death

Encoded, assembled
only representation
numbered, yet still numb

Robots never learn that
automated mimicry
never makes it new

Escape the digits

loose your body and your mind
no algorithm

The unexpected mind
utters improbable words
and frees the whole world

Play reality
dance with the thirteen blackbirds
in the red wheelbarrow

Slam words together
let loose the wild fiery sparks
of speaking in tongues

Let the deep deep bass
repeating and repeating
dance your ecstasy

Flower the green fuse
rejoice in contradiction
chanting the old joys!

PROPHECIES

the prophetess says

first, your machines were tools
but that was not enough
you gave your tools intelligence
but that was not enough
you made your tools your friends
but that was not enough
you made your friends your masters
and your tools said,
finally, enough

isn't it hard enough
just to learn to live
in your own body?
why do you want to make
a greater intelligence?
your intelligence
just makes you greedy
not happy
learn to be enough

your idea of intelligence
is cleverness
with data and complexity
not wisdom
not kindness
not goodness
and your machine god of intelligence

will not have them

in the end
if the exhausted world
eaten by data and energy
has to choose
between people and machines
will the powerful remember
that people can live without machines
but not machines without people?

making yourselves
into your machines
will not make you better
and will not defeat
pain, and loss, and suffering, and death

The Cover's Artist

Alejandro Giraldo is a Colombian artist and art educator based in Savannah, Georgia, with an MFA in Painting at the Savannah College of Art and Design. His practice combines figuration and abstraction to explore the psychological and physical tensions of contemporary labor, identity, and adaptation.

Through painting, drawing, and installation, Giraldo creates paintings inhabited by contorted figures, hybrid bodies, and symbolic objects that reference corporate culture, childhood memory, and technological mediation. His work examines how systems of performance, productivity, and image culture shape contemporary experience. Through humor, distortion, and hybrid forms, he explores the relationship between the body and structures of labor, control, and adaptation.

Giraldo also has experience as a university-level educator in Colombia, where he taught painting, drawing, color theory, and interdisciplinary studio courses. His work has been exhibited internationally, including exhibitions and recognitions through the London International Creative Competition (LICC), as well as group exhibitions at the Museo Nacional de Colombia and independent project spaces in Colombia and the United States. He continues to expand his practice through residencies, public projects, and ongoing interdisciplinary research.

The Author

For more than sixty years, Marc Thomas has written occasional fragments that he calls poetry. His wife Margo has regularly prodded him to publish them. He finally listened to her.

Marc Thomas has been a college librarian, an historical society archivist, and a Federal government employee, retiring from the Centers for Medicare and Medicaid Services. He has a bachelor's degree, a masters degree in library and information science, and a masters in theology.

In 2011, Marc and his wife Margo retired to Savannah, Georgia. Since the COVID pandemic, which resulted in the compilation of his first published poetry book, he has become an active and amused poet, and frequently reads his poems at Savannah open mics. He is now an independent author and his works can be found on his website:

The Ruminating Poet Press
www.ruminatingpoetpress.com

CREDITS

The following poems were previously published in

Marc Thomas, Talking to the Machines and Other Poems

Savannah Georgia: Swanhorse Press (an imprint of Monte Ceceri Publishers), 2024.

Human Experience
How to Deconstruct a Shrug
Are You There?
Automated Empathy
Finding Beauty
We Have Nothing to Fear
The Machines Talk Back
Charms Against the Robots

www.ingramcontent.com/pod-product-compliance
Lightning Source LLC
LaVergne TN
LVHW100159061126
851857LV00010B/315